Spotlight on Vocabulary

Roots, Prefixes and Suffixes

Carolyn LoGiudice and Kate LaQuay

Skill Areas:	Vocabulary
	Reading Comprehension
	Spelling
Ages:	9 through 13
Grades:	4 through 8

LinguiSystems, Inc.
3100 4th Avenue
East Moline, IL 61244-9700

FAX: 800-577-4555
E-mail: service@linguisystems.com
Web: linguisystems.com

800-776-4332

Copyright © 2005 LinguiSystems, Inc.

All of our products are copyrighted to protect the fine work of our authors. You may only copy the student materials as needed for your own use with students. Any other reproduction or distribution of the pages in this book is prohibited, including copying the entire book to use as another primary source or "master" copy.

Printed in the U.S.A.

ISBN 0-7606-0601-3

About the Authors

Carolyn LoGiudice

Carolyn LoGiudice, M.S., CCC-SLP, was a speech-language clinician in school, clinic, and private settings before joining LinguiSystems in 1984. She has co-authored many materials with LinguiSystems, including *The WORD Test*, *No-Glamour Vocabulary Cards*, *The Test of Semantic Skills (TOSS-P and TOSS-I)* and the *All-Star Vocabulary* game.

Kate and Michael LaQuay

Kate LaQuay, J.D., became part of LinguiSystems' extended family more than 20 years ago when her mother, Carolyn LoGiudice, joined the company. Now a mother herself, Kate has co-authored several LinguiSystems products, including *U.S. History: A Reading Comprehension Book*, *U.S. Government: A Reading Comprehension Game* and *Spotlight on Vocabulary: Levels 1 and 2*. Previously, she practiced law for six years in Los Angeles.

Dedication

For Michael, and the joy it will bring him to learn that words are just another playground

Illustrations by Margaret Warner

Cover Design by Mike Paustian

Table of Contents

Introduction 4
Pretest/Posttest 6
Root Words, Prefixes and Suffixes 7
Root Word Tips 8
Finding a Common Root 1 9
Finding a Common Root 2 10
Finding a Root Word 11
What Is a Prefix? 12
Finding a Word with a Prefix 13
Finding a Common Prefix 1 14
Finding a Common Prefix 2 15
Adding a Prefix to Make a Word 16
Using Prefixes to Build Words 1 *(un-, non-, dis-, in-, im-, ir-)* 17
Using Prefixes to Build Words 2 *(com-, co-, con-, sym-, syn-, sys-)* ... 18
Using Prefixes to Build Words 3 *(de-, anti-)* 19
Using Prefixes to Build Words 4 *(sub-, sus-)* 20
Using Prefixes to Build Words 5 *(pre-, pro-, ante-)* 21
Using Prefixes to Build Words 6 *(trans-, dia-)* 22
Using Prefixes to Build Words 7 *(contra-, dis-)* 23
Using Prefixes to Build Words 8 *(super-, hyper-, ultra-, over-)* 24
Using Prefixes to Build Words 9 *(retro-, re-)* 25
Writing Words with Prefixes *(review)* 26
What Is a Suffix? 27
Spelling Changes 28
Finding a Word with a Suffix 29
Grammar Suffixes 30
Noun Suffixes 1 *(-er, -or)* 31
Noun Suffixes 2 *(-ee)* 32
Noun Suffixes 3 *(-ness, -iness)* 33
Noun Suffixes 4 *(-ition, -ation)* 34
Adjective Suffixes 1 *(-less, -lessness)* 35
Adjective Suffixes 2 *(-ous, -ious, -eous, -ful)* 36
Adjective Suffixes 3 *(-ible, -able)* 37
Writing Words with Suffixes *(review)* 38
Answer Key 39

Spotlight on Vocabulary
Roots, Prefixes and Suffixes

Introduction

All students need to expand their working vocabularies. Some students have a natural facility for language and semantic relationships, enabling them to enlarge their vocabulary almost effortlessly. Simply reading, listening and talking seem to boost these students' vocabulary skills.

Many other students need to exert conscious energy to understand and recall an increasingly diverse vocabulary. Some of them are poor or reluctant readers. Other students have limited exposure to a rich variety of spoken English. Still others have language-learning disabilities, attention disorders or ineffective systems for storing and retrieving vocabulary. All of these students can benefit from specific vocabulary exposure and instruction. They can improve their vocabulary skills through conscious attention and guided learning.

The main goal of *Spotlight on Vocabulary* books is to help students recognize and use specific strategies to enrich their skills for understanding and using an increasingly rich vocabulary. *Word Roots, Prefixes and Suffixes* teaches students that many words are made up of smaller parts that have meaning and thus impact the total word. These are the student objectives of this book:

- To understand the function of a root or base word
- To identify a root word within a larger word
- To identify and understand the function of prefixes and suffixes
- To use root words, prefixes and suffixes to construct words

In this book, *root word* refers to the base or fundamental part of a word, such as *dance* in the word *dancing* or *nation* in the word *national*. The root of a word carries most of its meaning, but affixes can change root words into their opposites, change their intensity and sometimes make an entirely different word. This book demonstrates the power of affixes.

Some root words undergo spelling changes as certain prefixes or suffixes are added; other root words simply add prefixes or suffixes with no spelling changes. The activities in this book are sequenced by general complexity, and spelling changes are not specifically introduced until students begin the suffix section (page 27).

Here are some guidelines for doing the activities in this book with your students:

- Have your students take the Pretest/Posttest before they begin doing the activities in this book. When they have completed the book, have them retake the test and compare the results to their original scores.

- Teach your students to look for root (smaller) words within unfamiliar words. What is the smallest word within the word that makes a real word by itself? (An awareness of spelling changes with affixes comes in handy here.)

- Caution your students that affixes and root words do not always help us figure out what a word means, especially because word meanings change over time and as they become part of other languages. A dictionary is essential for determining and/or verifying definitions. Keep a student-friendly dictionary handy and encourage your students to consult it at any time while they're doing the activities.

- Before presenting a worksheet, write some words featuring the target affix on the board or an overhead. Ask your students to discover the common affix and to guess what it means. Then present the worksheet.

- Make a set of flash cards for prefixes and one for suffixes. List a suffix or prefix on one side and the meaning on the other. Have a small group of students take turns looking at a card and guessing the information on the back of a card.

- Make a list of affixes and root words (avoid ones with spelling changes unless your students can handle them). Write each root and affix on a separate card. Give one card to each student. Ask the students to build as many words as they can by linking with another student. Then as a group, list all the combinations discovered in this activity.

- Feature a root word or an affix for a week. Put a large sheet of paper on a bulletin board and have your students list as many words as they can that include the target.

- Encourage your students to be creative in making novel words that use affixes appropriately. A great way to start this concept is to have small groups of students brainstorm a fun name for a new product. Have each group design an ad for its product and present it to the class.

We hope *Roots, Prefixes and Suffixes* is a big hit with you and your students!

Carolyn and Kate

Pretest/Posttest

1. True or false? A **root word** has to do with gardening. _____

2. Circle the root word.   frosty   defrost   frosting   frost

3. Circle the root word.   subtract   add   division   multiply

4. What root do these words have in common?   taller   tallest   _____

5. Circle the root word for **gracious** and **graceful**.   full   grace   spacious

6. What is the prefix in the word **misleading**? _____

7. What is the suffix in the word **international**? _____

8. True or false? A root word has only one syllable. _____

9. Write a word with the prefix **mis-**. _____

10. Write a word with the suffix **-able**. _____

11. Write a word with the suffix **-ity**. _____

12. **Kindness** means being ___. _____

13. If something is **predictable**, you can ___ it. _____

14. The prefix **sub-** means ___. _____

15. The suffix **-less** means ___. _____

Spotlight on Vocabulary
Roots, Prefixes and Suffixes

Root Words, Prefixes and Suffixes

Many words are made up of small parts. If you know what the parts mean, you can make a good guess about what the whole word means. Think of the parts of the words in the box. Then guess what each one means.

The main part of a word that has small parts is the root of the word. In the word **previewing**, the root is **view**.

> overspending
> preadmission
> exhalation
> disconnection
> rerouted

You can **attach** or **fix** other parts to a root word to make a longer word.

A **prefix** is a part you add or fix **before** a root word.

root	prefix	new word
view	re-	review

Pre- means "before" and **-fix** means "attach." A **prefix** is a word part you **attach before a root word.**

A **suffix** is a part you add or fix **after** a root word.

root	prefix	new word
view	-ing	viewing

Suf- means "under" and **-fix** means "attach." A **suffix** is a word part you **attach to the end of a root word.**

Look carefully at each word below. Think about the parts of each word as you guess what each one means.

| outdweller | realignment | unpardoned | nonexistence |
| substructure | prejudgment | disrespect | interstate |

Spotlight on Vocabulary
Roots, Prefixes and Suffixes

Root Word Tips

A **word root** is the main part of a word. Here are some tips to learn about word roots.

- **Every word has at least one root in it.**
  Some words have two roots in them.

  sea   horse   seahorse

- **Some roots can stand alone as words.**

  school   fear   money   clear

- **You can add prefixes or suffixes to most root words to make other words with different meanings.**

  fear   fear**s**, fear**ed**, fear**ful**, **un**fear**ing**, fear**lessly**

  correct   correct**ly**, **in**correct, **in**correct**ly**, **un**correct**ed**

- **When you come to a word you don't know in what you read, look for the root word.** The root word will help you figure out what the word means.

Read the words in each row. Then underline the root word in each word.

1. decode   coded   codes   encode

2. disagree   agreement   agreed   disagreeable

3. disinterest   interesting   interestingly   uninterested

4. friendless   friendship   unfriendly   friendlier

5. unfold   folding   folders   folds

6. uncooked   cooking   overcooked   cooks

Spotlight on Vocabulary
Roots, Prefixes and Suffixes

Finding a Common Root ①

Circle the common root for the words in each row.

1. talking — talk — talks — talker

2. inaction — acting — act — action

3. addition — additional — add — added

4. unsuitable — suited — suitability — suit

5. limit — limitation — limited — unlimited

6. disorder — orderly — ordering — order

7. subtotal — totally — totaling — total

8. debrief — briefly — brief — briefing

9. civilization — uncivil — civil — civility

10. formality — informal — formally — formal

11. unequal — equally — equal — equalize

12. pleasant — pleasantly — unpleasant — pleasantness

Spotlight on Vocabulary
Roots, Prefixes and Suffixes

Finding a Common Root ②

Underline the root word that is common to both words in each pair.

1. kindness   unkind
2. conducting   conductor
3. uncover   covering
4. management   manages
5. unusual   usually
6. coastline   coastal
7. discomfort   uncomfortable
8. coauthor   authored
9. inaccurate   accurately
10. accomplishment   accomplished
11. loveliest   loveable
12. unreal   really

13. disappear   reappear
14. pavement   repave
15. prediction   predictable
16. unworthy   worthless
17. failure   failed
18. dismissed   dismissal
19. erupted   eruption
20. legalize   illegal
21. assistance   assisted
22. unblended   blending
23. disrespect   respectfully
24. honorable   dishonored

Spotlight on Vocabulary
Roots, Prefixes and Suffixes

Finding a Root Word

Circle the only root word in each row.

1. unpopular	proudly	purple	trying
2. originally	plural	independent	lately
3. ownership	subtraction	native	measurement
4. snarl	researcher	unaware	likely
5. remaining	rural	rigidly	frightening
6. reluctantly	straight	suburban	violently
7. unfortunate	requirement	wealth	supportive
8. policy	rebuild	instantly	submarine
9. incapable	final	inquiring	laborer
10. inclining	misunderstand	loyal	ideals
11. citizenship	bulge	disappoint	brilliantly
12. announcement	boastful	really	coast

Spotlight on Vocabulary
Roots, Prefixes and Suffixes

What Is a Prefix?

A **prefix** is a word part you add to the beginning of a word. Adding the prefix changes the meaning of the word.

root	prefix	new word
happy	un-	unhappy
play	re-	replay

Each prefix has a meaning. If you know what a prefix means, you can guess what an unfamiliar word with that prefix means. For example, the prefix **re-** means "again." If you see the word **regain**, you can guess it means "to gain again." In other words, to regain something means to get it back again.

If you learn what prefixes mean, you will boost your vocabulary skills. When you read a word you don't understand, look for the root word first.

    unfamiliar word — **antedate**

        root — **date** (means "when something happened")

Can you guess what the word means yet? Next look for a prefix.

    unfamiliar word — **antedate**

        prefix — **ante-** (means "before")

Now can you guess what the word means? It means "to happen before a date or time."

Read each group of words. The common prefix is in bold letters. Guess what each common prefix means.

1. **mis**place, **mis**fire, **mis**take, **mis**behave, **mis**guide
2. **un**do, **un**known, **un**seen, **un**happy, **un**clean
3. **pre**heat, **pre**war, **pre**order, **pre**shrink, **pre**mix
4. **dis**agree, **dis**comfort, **dis**please, **dis**color, **dis**courteous
5. **anti**war, **anti**freeze, **anti**theft, **anti**trust, **anti**glare

Spotlight on Vocabulary
Roots, Prefixes and Suffixes

Finding a Word with a Prefix

A **prefix** is a word part at the beginning of a word. If you take a prefix away, you change the meaning of the word that is left.

Underline each word that begins with a prefix.

1. My temperature is subnormal this morning.

2. Who won the contest this week?

3. Draw one semicircle with a line below it.

4. Kim used a secret chart to decode the message.

5. Would you rather read fiction or nonfiction books?

6. Our team won two intramural races this week.

7. If you disobey the law, you will be punished.

8. How many students were absent on Wednesday?

9. Mr. Lawrence can translate this chapter for us.

10. Jody filed a complaint about the smoke from the factory.

11. Let's get some snacks at intermission.

12. What time does your train depart from the station?

Spotlight on Vocabulary
Roots, Prefixes and Suffixes

Finding a Common Prefix ①

Find the common prefix in each row of words. Write the prefix in the blank.

1. submarine   subway   substitute   subtract   _____

2. prefer   prefix   predict   preview   _____

3. overtake   overthrow   overload   overnight   _____

4. recycle   reelect   refill   remind   _____

5. misplace   mistake   misjudge   mishap   _____

6. abnormal   absent   abbreviate   abrupt   _____

7. interrupt   interview   interpret   interfere   _____

8. translate   transfer   transplant   transport   _____

9. supernova   supervise   superficial   superhero   _____

10. ultrasuede ultramodern ultraviolet   ultrapure   _____

11. important   immature   immoral   immune   _____

12. exhale   explode   exit   exhaust   _____

Spotlight on Vocabulary
Roots, Prefixes and Suffixes

Finding a Common Prefix ②

Find the common prefix in each row of words. Write the prefix in the blank.

1. provide   protest   proceed   proclaim   _____

2. detach   descend   deform   decline   _____

3. semicircle   semicolon   semiskilled   semidarkness   _____

4. antihistamine   antibody   antifreeze   antibiotic   _____

5. compass   compound   compose   complete   _____

6. conduct   concentrate   connect   confess   _____

7. disguise   dislike   dishonest   disagree   _____

8. impossible   imply   imperfect   immortal   _____

9. subdue   subject   submit   subscribe   _____

10. replace   reply   recheck   refund   _____

11. untie   unfold   unknown   uncover   _____

12. prewash   precede   prepare   premature   _____

Spotlight on Vocabulary
Roots, Prefixes and Suffixes

Adding a Prefix to Make a Word

Add a prefix from the box to change each word into a new word that makes sense. You will use some prefixes more than once.

ab-	dis-	mis-	re-	inter-
pre-	super-	un-	com-	pro-

1. _____hero

2. _____normal

3. _____national

4. _____caution

5. _____guide

6. _____gust

7. _____peat

8. _____plain

9. _____pose

10. _____spoken

11. _____rupt

12. _____like

13. _____vide

14. _____hook

15. _____pare

Spotlight on Vocabulary
Roots, Prefixes and Suffixes

Using Prefixes to Build Words 1

Each prefix in the box means **not** or **the opposite of**. Choose a prefix from the box to add to each word below. Then, on a separate sheet of paper, write what each new word means.

un-	dis-	im-
non-	in-	ir-

1. _____able
2. _____mature
3. _____vent
4. _____sense
5. _____aware
6. _____afraid
7. _____correct
8. _____possible
9. _____regular

10. _____certain
11. _____dairy
12. _____appear
13. _____responsible
14. _____complete
15. _____proper
16. _____honest
17. _____fat
18. _____pure

Spotlight on Vocabulary
Roots, Prefixes and Suffixes

Using Prefixes to Build Words ②

Each prefix in the box means **with** or **together**. Choose a prefix from the box to add to each root word below. (You may use a prefix more than once.) Then write what each new word means.

> com-   con-   syn-
> co-   sym-   sys-

Tip: Some of these root words do not make real words without a prefix.

1. _____plete   _____

2. _____bine   _____

3. _____operate   _____

4. _____phony   _____

5. _____pathy   _____

6. _____tact   _____

7. _____thetic   _____

8. _____tem   _____

9. _____onym   _____

10. _____bolize   _____

11. _____metry   _____

12. _____cern   _____

Spotlight on Vocabulary
Roots, Prefixes and Suffixes

Using Prefixes to Build Words ③

Each prefix in the box means **away from**, **against**, or **the opposite of**. Choose a prefix from the box to add to each root word below. (You may use a prefix more than once.) Then write what each new word means.

> de-   anti-

Tip: Some of these root words do not make real words without a prefix.

1. _____mote   _____

2. _____crease   _____

3. _____freeze   _____

4. _____port   _____

5. _____war   _____

6. _____part   _____

7. _____frost   _____

8. _____biotic   _____

9. _____body   _____

10. _____code   _____

11. _____odorant   _____

12. _____scend   _____

Spotlight on Vocabulary
Roots, Prefixes and Suffixes

Using Prefixes to Build Words ④

Each prefix in the box means **under** or **below**. Choose a prefix from the box to add to each root word below. (You may use a prefix more than once.) Then write what each new word means.

> sub-   sus-

Tip: Some of these root words do not make real words without a prefix.

1. _____marine _____

2. _____scription _____

3. _____pect _____

4. _____merge _____

5. _____mit _____

6. _____stitute _____

7. _____tract _____

8. _____way _____

9. _____pend _____

10. _____urb _____

11. _____tain _____

12. _____pense _____

Spotlight on Vocabulary
Roots, Prefixes and Suffixes

Using Prefixes to Build Words ⑤

Each prefix in the box means **before** or **below**. Choose a prefix from the box to add to each root word below. (You may use a prefix more than once.) Then write what each new word means.

> pre-   pro-   ante-

Tip: Some of these root words do not make real words without a prefix.

1. _____duce _____

2. _____vent _____

3. _____cession _____

4. _____dict _____

5. _____pare _____

6. _____face _____

7. _____room _____

8. _____view _____

9. _____test _____

10. _____ceed _____

11. _____vide _____

12. _____fade _____

Spotlight on Vocabulary
Roots, Prefixes and Suffixes

Using Prefixes to Build Words ⑥

Each prefix in the box means **through** or **across**. Choose a prefix from the box to add to each root word below. (You may use a prefix more than once.) Then write what each new word means.

> trans-   dia-

Tip: Some of these root words do not make real words without a prefix.

1. _____meter _____

2. _____port _____

3. _____fer _____

4. _____gonal _____

5. _____lect _____

6. _____parent _____

7. _____gram _____

8. _____gnosis _____

9. _____form _____

10. _____late _____

11. _____action _____

12. _____fusion _____

Spotlight on Vocabulary
Roots, Prefixes and Suffixes

Using Prefixes to Build Words 7

Each prefix in the box means **against** or **opposing**. Choose a prefix from the box to add to each root word below. (You may use a prefix more than once.) Then write what each new word means.

> contra-   dis-

Tip: Some of these root words do not make real words without a prefix.

1. _____grace   _____

2. _____dict   _____

3. _____satisfy _____

4. _____miss   _____

5. _____continue _____

6. _____dictory _____

7. _____locate _____

8. _____belief _____

9. _____charge _____

10. _____loyal   _____

11. _____appear _____

12. _____card   _____

Spotlight on Vocabulary Roots, Prefixes and Suffixes

Using Prefixes to Build Words ⑧

Each prefix in the box means **over** or **excessive**. Choose a prefix from the box to add to each root word below. (You may use a prefix more than once.) Then write what each new word means.

> super-   ultra-
> hyper-   over-

Tip: Some of these root words do not make real words without a prefix.

1. _____sensitive _____

2. _____aged _____

3. _____suede _____

4. _____cast _____

5. _____look _____

6. _____take _____

7. _____natural _____

8. _____stition _____

9. _____sleep _____

10. _____modern _____

11. _____violet _____

12. _____cook _____

Spotlight on Vocabulary
Roots, Prefixes and Suffixes

Using Prefixes to Build Words ⑨

Each prefix in the box means **again** or **back**. Choose a prefix from the box to add to each root word below. (You may use a prefix more than once.) Then write what each new word means.

> retro-   re-

Tip: Some of these root words do not make real words without a prefix.

1. _____do   _____

2. _____active   _____

3. _____made   _____

4. _____vise   _____

5. _____gain   _____

6. _____fit   _____

7. _____gress   _____

8. _____mind   _____

9. _____call   _____

10. _____fill   _____

11. _____new   _____

12. _____cite   _____

Spotlight on Vocabulary
Roots, Prefixes and Suffixes

Writing Words with Prefixes

List at least three words that begin with each prefix.

re- non- pre-

dis- trans- un-

sub- pro- com-

What Is a Suffix?

A **suffix** is a word part you add to the end of a word. Each suffix has its own meaning. When you add a suffix to a root word, you change the meaning of the whole word.

root	suffix	new word
paint	-er	painter
inform	-ation	information

You can add different suffixes to the same base word. Each new word means something different. Look at these words from the root word **act**.

suffix	new word	meaning
-or	actor	one who acts
-ion	action	movement
-ing	acting	playing a role
-ive	active	lively
-ivity	activity	a task or the state of being active
-ivator	activator	one who starts an action or makes something move

Read each group of words. The common suffix is in bold letters. Guess what each common suffix means.

1. climb**ing**, think**ing**, laugh**ing**, sleep**ing**, read**ing**
2. port**able**, comfort**able**, love**able**, drink**able**, break**able**
3. fear**less**, care**less**, point**less**, sleep**less**, taste**less**
4. book**s**, clip**s**, dove**s**, cloud**s**, tree**s**
5. rough**ness**, smooth**ness**, hard**ness**, good**ness**, well**ness**
6. thought**ful**, care**ful**, wake**ful**, art**ful**, grace**ful**
7. pian**ist**, chem**ist**, flor**ist**, flut**ist**, dent**ist**

Spotlight on Vocabulary
Roots, Prefixes and Suffixes

Spelling Changes

Sometimes you have to change the spelling at the end of the root word when you add a suffix. Whenever you aren't sure how to spell a word, use a dictionary to check the spelling.

Here are some spelling rules that will help you make good guesses about spelling words with suffixes.

- **Drop a final -e before a suffix that starts with a vowel.**

    share + -ing = sharing

    sense + -ible = sensible

    Exception: If a root word ends with a soft *c* or *g* before final *-e* and you want to add a suffix that starts with *a* or *o*, keep the final *-e* of the root word.

    courage + -ous = courageous   trace + -able = traceable

- **Keep a final -e before a suffix that starts with a consonant.**

    brave + -ly = bravely   hope + -fully = hopefully

- **If a root word ends with a consonant + -y, change the -y to -i before any suffix except one that starts with -i.**

    deny + -able = deniable   hurry + -ing = hurrying

    merry + -ly = merrily   lobby + -ist = lobbyist

- **If a root word ends in a single vowel plus a consonant and is one syllable or the last syllable is accented, double the final consonant before a suffix that starts with a vowel.**

    set + -ing = setting   submit + -er = submitter

    control + -able = controllable   thin + -est = thinnest

    refer + -ing = referring   refer + -ence = reference (accent changes)

Look at these words. Underline each word that shows a spelling change when a suffix was added to it.

preference	hiking	reliable	national	nicely	totally
prettily	knowing	activity	creator	lovely	smiling

Spotlight on Vocabulary
Roots, Prefixes and Suffixes

Finding a Word with a Suffix

A **suffix** is a word part at the end of a word. If you take a suffix away, you change the meaning of the word that is left.

Underline each word that ends with a suffix.

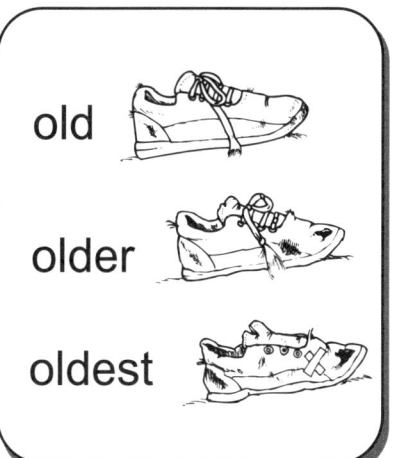

old
older
oldest

1. Keith wore his oldest shoes to the picnic.

2. The Kwong family will soon move to a new location.

3. Are all mushrooms poisonous?

4. The musician practiced for hours at a time.

5. Be friendly if you expect to have more friends.

6. Brenda told a spooky story with a happy ending.

7. How many people live in your neighborhood?

8. Joel is bashful when he has to perform in public.

9. Use your calculator to do the division more quickly.

10. Who has the highest singing voice in the choir?

11. Ahmed created a beautiful garden with many flowering plants.

12. Some of your sarcastic remarks were hurtful.

13. Be sensible about getting enough sleep each night.

Grammar Suffixes

Some suffixes are grammar signals. They tell you things like plurals or verb tenses. Here are some examples.

The suffixes **-s** and **-es** make words plural.   rabbit + -s = rabbits
wish + -es = wishes

The suffix **-ed** shows the past tense of a verb.   kick + -ed = kicked
laugh + -ed = laughed

The suffix **-ing** shows the present tense or a noun made from a verb.   swim + -ing = swimming
relax + -ing = relaxing

The suffixes **-er** and **-est** show comparisons.   strong + -er = stronger (more strong)
strong + -est = strongest (most strong)

Underline each word that has a grammar suffix.

1. Ken was awarded three ribbons for his prize pig.

2. Which are easier to clean, your hands or your feet?

3. We're watching movies tonight with some friends.

4. Ted wrapped the present and placed two bows on top.

5. We climbed higher today than we ever climbed before.

6. My aunt married a columnist for two national newspapers.

7. These math problems are trickier than I thought.

8. We walked along the water and looked for pretty shells.

9. We used the widest ribbon to make bows around the trees.

Noun Suffixes 1

Some suffixes turn root words into nouns. For example, the suffix **-or** turns the verb **act** into **actor**—someone who acts. The suffix **-er** turns the verb **produce** into **producer**—someone who produces something.

-er   **-or**

Finish these sentences to explain the words in bold print.

1. An **employer** is someone who _____.

2. A **buyer** is someone who _____.

3. A **teacher** is someone who _____.

4. A **manager** is someone who _____.

5. A **thinker** is someone who _____.

6. A **believer** is someone who _____.

7. A **blamer** is someone who _____.

8. A **challenger** is someone who _____.

9. A **builder** is someone who _____.

10. A **commander** is someone who _____.

11. A **conductor** is someone who _____.

12. A **dreamer** is someone who _____.

13. A **dieter** is someone who _____.

14. A **director** is someone who _____.

Spotlight on Vocabulary
Roots, Prefixes and Suffixes

Noun Suffixes 2

The suffix **-ee** means someone who receives the action of the root word (verb). For example, a **trainee** *(train + -ee)* is someone who is being trained.

Finish these sentences to explain the words in bold print.

1. An **employee** is someone who is _____.

2. An **interviewee** is someone who is _____.

3. A **nominee** is someone who is _____.

4. A **detainee** is someone who is _____.

5. A **licensee** is someone who is _____.

6. A **trustee** is someone who is _____.

7. An **escapee** is someone who is _____.

8. An **evacuee** is someone who is _____.

9. An **appointee** is someone who is _____.

10. A **selectee** is someone who is _____.

11. A **returnee** is someone who is _____.

12. An **absentee** is someone who is _____.

13. An **electee** is someone who is _____.

14. A **rejectee** is someone who is _____.

Spotlight on Vocabulary
Roots, Prefixes and Suffixes

Noun Suffixes ③

The suffixes **-ness** and **-iness** mean a state or a condition of the root word (usually an adjective). For example, **happiness** *(happy + -ness)* means "being happy."

-ness   -iness

Finish these sentences to explain the words in bold print.

1. **Saltiness** means being _____.

2. **Gladness** means being _____.

3. **Boldness** means being _____.

4. **Sadness** means being _____.

5. **Thirstiness** means being _____.

6. **Loneliness** means being _____.

7. **Attractiveness** means being _____.

8. **Friendliness** means being _____.

9. **Strangeness** means being _____.

10. **Helplessness** means being _____.

11. **Fairness** means being _____.

12. **Emptiness** means being _____.

13. **Thoughtfulness** means being _____.

14. **Cleverness** means being _____.

*Spotlight on Vocabulary
Roots, Prefixes and Suffixes*

Noun Suffixes ④

The suffixes **-ition** and **-ation** can change verb root words into nouns. For example, **imagination** *(imagine + -ation)* is the act of imaging.

-ition   **-ation**

Finish these sentences to explain the words in bold print.

1. **Declaration** is the act of _____.

2. **Addition** is the act of _____.

3. **Association** is the act of _____.

4. **Classification** is the act of _____.

5. **Combination** is the act of _____.

6. **Education** is the act of _____.

7. **Competition** is the act of _____.

8. **Conservation** is the act of _____.

9. **Conversation** is the act of _____.

10. **Communication** is the act of _____.

11. **Multiplication** is the act of _____.

12. **Recognition** is the act of _____.

13. **Evaporation** is the act of _____.

14. **Observation** is the act of _____.

Adjective Suffixes ①

The suffix **-less** means "without" or "lacking" the root word. For example, **toothless** *(tooth + -less)* means "without teeth."

-less

Finish these sentences to explain the words in bold print.

1. **Sleepless** means without _____.

2. **Hopeless** means without _____.

3. **Defenseless** means without _____.

4. **Endless** means without _____.

5. **Thoughtless** means without _____.

6. **Careless** means without _____.

7. **Sugarless** means without _____.

8. **Lawless** means without _____.

9. **Errorless** means without _____.

10. **Countless** means without _____.

11. **Blameless** means without _____.

12. **Doubtless** means without _____.

13. **Senseless** means without _____.

14. **Fearless** means without _____.

Spotlight on Vocabulary
Roots, Prefixes and Suffixes

Adjective Suffixes ②

The suffixes **-ous**, **-ious**, **-eous**, and **-ful** usually signal adjectives that mean "having" or "full of" the root word. For example, **thoughtful** *(thought + ful)* means "full of thought" and **religious** *(religion + -ous)* means "having religion."

> -ous   -ious   -eous   -ful

Write the letters in the blanks to match the words on the left to the root words on the right.

1. _____ cancerous   A. beauty
2. _____ dangerous   B. cancer
3. _____ cautious   C. caution
4. _____ righteous   D. danger
5. _____ repetitious   E. doubt
6. _____ fictitious   F. fame
7. _____ poisonous   G. fiction
8. _____ doubtful   H. grace
9. _____ famous   I. mountain
10. _____ mountainous   J. mystery
11. _____ mysterious   K. poison
12. _____ beauteous   L. repeat
13. _____ gracious   M. resource
14. _____ resourceful   N. right

Spotlight on Vocabulary Roots, Prefixes and Suffixes

Adjective Suffixes ③

The suffixes **-ible** and **-able** can signal adjectives that mean "able to be" the root word. For example, **washable** *(wash + -able)* means "able to be washed."

-ible   -able

Finish these sentences to explain the words in bold print.

1. You can _____ something that is **breakable**.

2. You can _____ something that is **recyclable**.

3. You can _____ something that is **noticeable**.

4. You can _____ something that is **reversible**.

5. You can _____ something that is **divisible**.

6. You can _____ something that is **enjoyable**.

7. You can _____ something that is **payable**.

8. You can _____ something that is **defensible**.

9. You can _____ something that is **erasable**.

10. You can _____ something that is **readable**.

11. You can _____ something that is **comparable**.

12. You can _____ something that is **controllable**.

13. You can _____ something that is **collectible**.

14. You can _____ something that is **stretchable**.

*Spotlight on Vocabulary
Roots, Prefixes and Suffixes*

Writing Words with Suffixes

List at least three words that end with each suffix.

-ly	-less	-ful
_____	_____	_____
_____	_____	_____
_____	_____	_____
_____	_____	_____

-or	-ee	-ness
_____	_____	_____
_____	_____	_____
_____	_____	_____
_____	_____	_____

-ation	-ous	-able
_____	_____	_____
_____	_____	_____
_____	_____	_____
_____	_____	_____

Spotlight on Vocabulary
Roots, Prefixes and Suffixes

Answer Key

The most likely answers are listed here. Accept other logical, appropriate answers as correct.

Page 6
1. false
2. frost
3. add
4. tall
5. grace
6. mis-
7. -al, -tional
8. false
9. Answers vary.
10. Answers vary.
11. Answers vary.
12. kind
13. predict
14. under, below
15. without, opposite

Page 8
1. code
2. agree
3. interest
4. friend
5. fold
6. cook

Page 9
1. talk
2. act
3. add
4. suit
5. limit
6. order
7. total
8. brief
9. civil
10. formal
11. equal
12. pleasant

Page 10
1. kind
2. conduct
3. cover
4. manage
5. usual
6. coast
7. comfort
8. author
9. accurate
10. accomplish
11. love
12. real
13. appear
14. pave
15. predict
16. worth
17. fail
18. dismiss
19. erupt
20. legal
21. assist
22. blend
23. respect
24. honor

Page 11
1. purple
2. plural
3. native
4. snarl
5. rural
6. straight
7. wealth
8. policy
9. final
10. loyal
11. bulge
12. coast

Page 12
1. not, ill, wrongly
2. reverse, not
3. before
4. negative, not
5. opposing, preventing

Page 13
1. subnormal
2. contest
3. semicircle
4. decode
5. nonfiction
6. intramural
7. disobey
8. absent
9. translate
10. complaint
11. intermission
12. depart

Page 14
1. sub-
2. pre-
3. over-
4. re-
5. mis-
6. ab-
7. inter-
8. trans-
9. super-
10. ultra-
11. im-
12. ex-

Page 15
1. pro-
2. de-
3. semi-
4. anti-
5. com-
6. con-
7. dis-
8. im-
9. sub-
10. re-
11. un-
12. pre-

Page 16
1. superhero
2. abnormal
3. international
4. precaution, recaution
5. misguide, reguide
6. disgust
7. repeat
8. complain
9. dispose, compose, propose
10. misspoken, unspoken
11. interrupt, disrupt
12. dislike, unlike
13. provide
14. unhook
15. compare, prepare

Page 17
1. unable, disable; not able, to make unable
2. immature; not mature, juvenile
3. invent; to create
4. nonsense; silliness
5. unaware; not knowing
6. unafraid; not afraid
7. incorrect; not correct, wrong
8. impossible; not possible
9. irregular; uneven, not regular
10. uncertain; not certain, doubtful
11. nondairy; without dairy products
12. disappear; fade from view
13. irresponsible; not responsible
14. incomplete; not complete
15. improper; not proper, incorrect
16. dishonest; not honest
17. nonfat; without fat
18. impure; not pure

Page 18
1. complete; done, to finish, finished
2. combine; to mix
3. cooperate; to work together
4. symphony; a musical piece
5. sympathy; pity
6. contact; touch
7. synthetic; fake, artificial
8. system; program
9. synonym; word that means the same thing
10. symbolize; to represent
11. symmetry; balance
12. concern; worry

Page 19
1. demote; to give a lower job/rank
2. decrease; to shrink
3. antifreeze; keeps from freezing
4. deport; to expel
5. antiwar; against war
6. depart; to leave
7. defrost; to melt
8. antibiotic; drug to kill bacteria
9. antibody; attacks virus
10. decode; to translate
11. deodorant; keeps odor away
12. descend; to go down

Page 20
1. submarine; below the sea
2. subscription; agreement to pay for issues
3. suspect; a person under suspicion
4. submerge; to go below water
5. submit; to give up to some authority
6. substitute; to take the place of
7. subtract; to take away
8. subway; a way underground
9. suspend; to hold up or withhold
10. suburban; a living area outside of a city
11. sustain; to continue, suffer
12. suspense; not knowing what will happen

Page 21
1. produce; to cause or make
2. prevent; to keep from happening
3. procession; the act of moving along
4. predict; to forecast

Spotlight on Vocabulary
Roots, Prefixes and Suffixes

Page 21, continued
5. prepare; to make ready
6. preface; an introductory statement
7. anteroom; a waiting room
8. preview; to view in advance
9. pretest; to test in advance
10. proceed; to go forth
11. provide; to give or equip
12. prefade; to fade before using

Page 22
1. diameter; a line across
2. transport; to move
3. transfer; to switch
4. diagonal; oblique
5. dialect; a language variant
6. transparent; sheer, able to be seen through
7. diagram; a chart or drawing
8. diagnosis; a description
9. transform; to change
10. translate; to convert
11. transaction; an interaction
12. transfusion; a transfer

Page 23
1. disgrace; loss of respect
2. contradict; to deny or say the opposite
3. dissatisfy; to not please
4. dismiss; to let go
5. discontinue; to stop or end
6. contradictory; opposing
7. dislocate; to put out of place
8. disbelief; unbelief
9. discharge; to fire or let go
10. disloyal; not loyal
11. disappear; to vanish
12. discard; to get rid of

Page 24
1. hypersensitive, oversensitive; too sensitive
2. overaged; too old
3. ultrasuede; suedelike fabric
4. overcast; cloudy
5. overlook; to not notice
6. overtake; to pass
7. supernatural; not natural
8. superstition; a nonfactual belief
9. oversleep; to sleep too long
10. ultramodern; very current
11. ultraviolet; longer than X-rays
12. overcook; to cook too long

Page 25
1. redo; to do again
2. retroactive; applying to the past
3. remade; made again
4. revise; to change
5. regain; to gain again
6. refit; to equip old machines with new parts
7. regress; to return
8. remind; to bring back to mind
9. recall; to remember
10. refill; to fill again
11. renew; to make new again
12. recite; to say from memory

Page 26
Answers will vary.

Page 27
1. in the act of
2. able to be
3. without
4. plural
5. having the quality of
6. full of
7. one who

Page 28
hiking, reliable, prettily, activity, creator, smiling

Page 29
1. oldest, shoes
2. location
3. mushrooms, poisonous
4. musician, practiced, hours
5. friendly, friends
6. spooky, ending
7. neighborhood
8. bashful
9. calculator, division, quickly
10. highest, singing
11. created, beautiful, flowering, plants
12. sarcastic, remarks, hurtful
13. sensible, getting

Page 30
1. awarded, ribbons
2. easier, hands
3. watching, movies, friends
4. wrapped, placed, bows
5. climbed, higher, climbed
6. married, columnist, national, newspapers
7. problems, trickier
8. walked, looked, shells
9. used, widest, bows, trees

Page 31
1. employs
2. buys
3. teaches
4. manages
5. thinks
6. believes
7. blames
8. challenges
9. builds
10. commands
11. conducts
12. dreams
13. diets
14. directs

Page 32
1. employed
2. interviewed
3. nominated
4. detained
5. licensed
6. trusted
7. escaping, has escaped
8. evacuating, has evacuated
9. appointed
10. selected
11. returning, has returned
12. absent
13. elected
14. rejected

Page 33
1. salty
2. glad
3. bold
4. sad
5. thirsty
6. lonely
7. attractive
8. friendly
9. strange
10. helpless
11. fair
12. empty
13. thoughtful
14. clever

Page 34
1. declaring
2. adding
3. associating
4. classifying
5. combining
6. educating
7. competing
8. conserving
9. conversing
10. communicating
11. multiplying
12. recognizing
13. evaporating
14. observing

Page 35
1. sleep
2. hope
3. defense
4. end
5. thought
6. care
7. sugar
8. law
9. error
10. count
11. blame
12. doubt
13. sense
14. fear

Page 36
1. B   8. E
2. D   9. F
3. C   10. I
4. N   11. J
5. L   12. A
6. G   13. H
7. K   14. M

Page 37
1. break
2. recycle
3. notice
4. reverse
5. divide
6. enjoy
7. pay
8. defend
9. erase
10. read
11. compare
12. control
13. collect
14. stretch

Page 38
Answers will vary.